MW01073977

WHOSE
HAIR?

CHRISTINA CHRISTOFOROU

LAURENCE KING PUBLISHING

LAURENCE KING

Published in 2011 by
Laurence King Publishing Ltd
361–373 City Road
London EC1V 1LR
United Kingdom
Tel: +44 20 7841 6900
Fax: +44 20 7841 6910
e-mail: enquiries@laurenceking.com
www.laurenceking.com

A catalogue record for this book is
available from the British Library.

ISBN 978-1-85669-715-6

Book and cover design by & SMITH
www.andsmithdesign.com
Illustration: Christina Christoforou
Senior Editor: Melissa Danny

Printed in China

I'VE ALWAYS CONSIDERED A 'BAD HAIR DAY' TO BE A SMALL DISASTER.
IT'S LIKE NOT BEING QUITE YOURSELF.

WHILE DRAWING THE HAIRSTYLES OF THE PEOPLE IN THIS BOOK,
I COULDN'T HELP BUT THINK OF THE STATEMENT THAT EACH
HAIRSTYLE MAKES AND HOW, BECAUSE OF THIS, A FEATURE AS TRIVIAL
AS HAIR BECOMES PART OF THAT PERSON'S IDENTITY AND WHY WE
RECOGNIZE THEM. IN MY EYES, JIMI HENDRIX'S HAIRSTYLE SAYS 'FREEDOM',
ANNA WINTOUR'S SAYS 'DISCIPLINE', JEAN-MICHEL BASQUIAT'S 'IMAGINATION',
AUDREY HEPBURN'S 'ELEGANCE', RUSSELL BRAND'S 'ACT',
AMY WINEHOUSE'S 'DRAMA', AND SO ON.

AFTER OVER 200 DRAWINGS OF FAMOUS HAIR,
I AM CONTEMPLATING THE IDEA THAT PEOPLE, MORE OFTEN THAN NOT,
ARE EXACTLY WHO THEY APPEAR TO BE.

CHRISTINA CHRISTOFOROU, 2011

MUSIC

FILM COUPLES/FAMILY

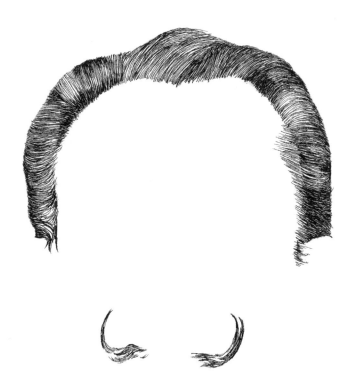

TV SERIES COUPLES

PHILOSOPHY

TV SERIES COUPLES

TV SERIES COUPLES

ART

POP STARS

POLITICS/FAMILY

MUSIC/FILM

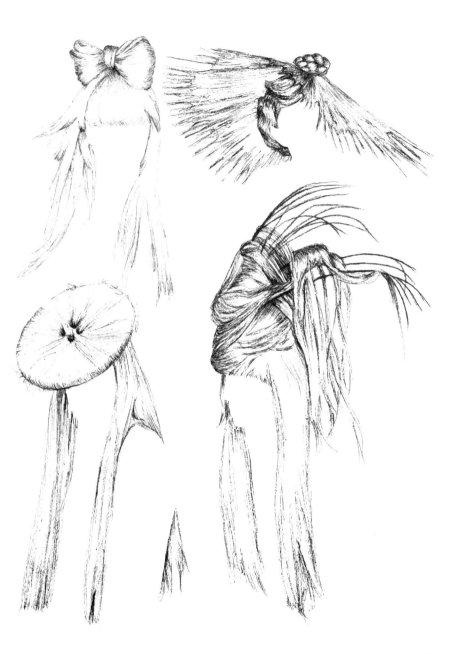

SPORT

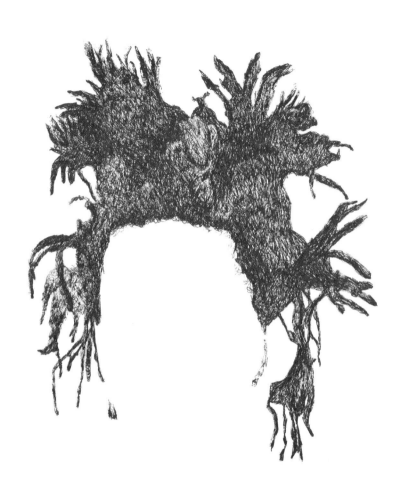

SPORT

REVOLUTIONARIES

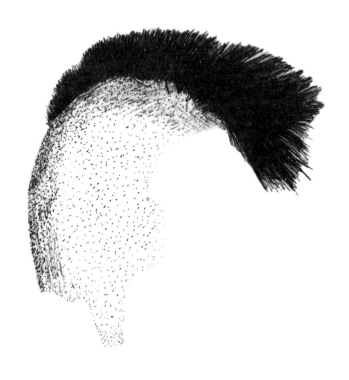

FILM CHARACTERS

ROYALTY

GUITAR LEGENDS

POP STARS

FILM CHARACTERS

COMEDY

SPORT

TV SERIES CHARACTERS

POLITICS

MUSIC

FASHION

POLITICS

POP STARS

TV SERIES CHARACTERS

SPORT

SCIENCE

FILM CHARACTERS

SPORT

FILM CHARACTERS

FILM CHARACTERS

FILM CHARACTERS

FILM CHARACTERS

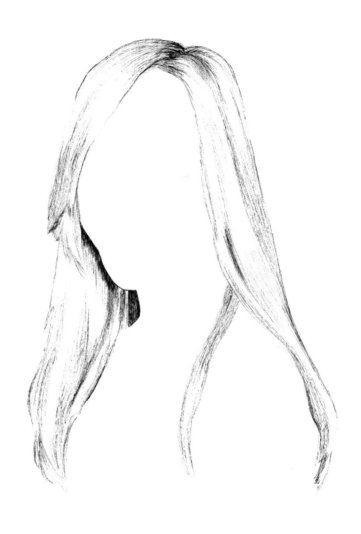

BUSINESS MAGNATES

POP STARS

FASHION

SPORT

CHEFS

FILM COUPLES/FAMILY

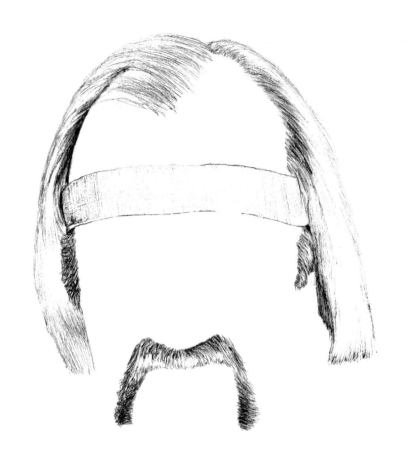

SPORT/FILM

FILM COUPLES

REVOLUTIONARIES/ACTIVISTS

FILM CHARACTERS

FILM CHARACTERS

POETRY/THEATRE

COMEDY

MUSIC

FILM CHARACTERS

LIFESTYLE GURU

TV SERIES CHARACTERS

TV SERIES CHARACTERS

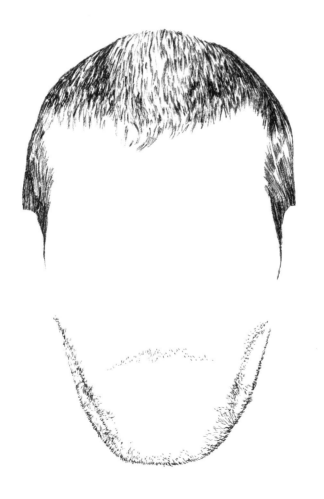

SPORT

SPORT

ART

MUSIC

MUSIC

4 – MUSIC
Bruce Springsteen

11 – FILM COUPLES
Sandy Ollson & Danny Zuko in Grease

18 – POP STARS
Madonna

5 – SPORT
Björn Borg (tennis)

12 – PHILOSOPHY
Friedrich Nietzsche

19 – POLITICS/ FAMILY
Nicolas Sarkozy & Carla Bruni

6 – FILM COUPLES/FAMILY
Brad Pitt & Angelina Jolie

13 – SCIENCE
Albert Einstein

20 – POLITICS/ FAMILY
Barack, Michelle, Sasha & Malia Obama

7 – SPORT
David Beckham (football)

14 – TV SERIES COUPLES
Rachel & Ross of Friends

21 – MUSIC
Elvis Presley

8 – ART
Salvador Dalí

15 – TV SERIES COUPLES
Carrie & Mr Big of Sex & the City

22 – MUSIC/FILM
Grace Jones

9 – COMEDY
Charlie Chaplin

16 – ART
Frida Kahlo

23 – POP STARS
Lady Gaga

10 – TV SERIES COUPLES
Agent Mulder & Agent Scully of The X Files

17 – FILM CHARACTERS
Sean Connery, George Lazenby, Roger Moore, Timothy Dalton, Pierce Brosnan & Daniel Craig in James Bond

24 – SPORT
Cristiano Ronaldo (football)

25 – SPORT
George Foreman
& Muhammad Ali
(boxing)

**32 – REVOLU-
TIONARIES**
Che Guevara

39 – FASHION
Mary Quant

**26 – GUITAR
LEGENDS**
Slash

33 – FASHION
John Galliano

40 – POP STARS
Victoria Adams,
Melanie Brown,
Melanie Chisholm,
Emma Bunton &
Geri Halliwell of
The Spice Girls

27 – FASHION
Kate Moss

**34 – FILM
CHARACTERS**
Robert De Niro
in Taxi Driver

41 – MUSIC
John Lennon,
George Harrison,
Paul McCartney &
Ringo Starr of The
Beatles

28 – ART
Jean-Michel
Basquiat

**35 – FILM
CHARACTERS**
James Dean in
Rebel Without
a Cause

**42 – FILM
CHARACTERS**
Emma Watson,
Rupert Grint &
Daniel Radcliffe in
Harry Potter

**29 – BUSINESS
MAGNATES**
Donald Trump

36 – ROYALTY
Princess Diana

43 – DICTATORS
Adolf Hitler,
Mao Zedong &
Joseph Stalin

30 – SPORT
Ayrton Senna
(motor racing)

**37 – TV/ACTING/
COMEDY**
Russell Brand

44 – COMEDY
Larry David

31 – FASHION
Karl Lagerfeld

**38 – GUITAR
LEGENDS**
Jimi Hendrix

45 – TV
Simon Cowell

46 – SPORT
Didier Drogba
(football)

53 – MUSIC
Bob Marley

**60 – TV SERIES
CHARACTERS**
Jennifer Saunders
& Joanna Lumley
in Absolutely
Fabulous

**47 – BUSINESS
MAGNATES**
Richard Branson

54 – FASHION
Anna Wintour

61 – SCIENCE
Charles Darwin

**48 – TV SERIES
CHARACTERS**
Mad Men

55 – MUSIC
David Bowie

62 – SPORT
Diego Maradona
(football)

49 – ART
Vincent van Gogh

56 – POLITICS
Margaret Thatcher

63 – POP STARS
Michael Jackson

50 – POLITICS
Abraham Lincoln

57 – POLITICS
Ronald Reagan

64 – TV
Oprah Winfrey

**51 – FILM
CHARACTERS**
Brigitte Bardot in
And God Created
Woman

58 – POP STARS
Howie Dorough,
Nick Carter,
Kevin Richardson,
Brian Littrell &
A.J. McLean of
Backstreet Boys

**65 – TV SERIES
CHARACTERS**
Eva Longoria,
Marcia Cross, Teri
Hatcher & Felicity
Huffman in
Desperate
Housewives

52 – MUSIC
Beyoncé

59 – MUSIC
Lars Ulrich,
James Hetfield,
Kirk Hammett &
Jason Newsted of
Metallica

66 – SCIENCE
Sigmund Freud

67 – MUSIC
Amy Winehouse

74 – FILM CHARACTERS
Audrey Hepburn in Breakfast at Tiffany's

81 – FASHION
Coco Chanel

68 – FILM CHARACTERS
Steve McQueen in Bullitt

75 – DIRECTORS
Tim Burton, Orson Welles, Stanley Kubrick, David Lynch, Woody Allen, Quentin Tarantino & Steven Spielberg

82 – BUSINESS MAGNATES
Bill Gates

69 – SPORT
Andre Agassi (tennis)

76 – FILM CHARACTERS
Robert Redford & Paul Newman in Butch Cassidy & The Sundance Kid

83 – PHILOSOPHY
Karl Marx

70 – MUSIC
Anni-Frid Lyngstad, Björn Ulvaeus, Benny Andersson & Agnetha Fältskog of ABBA

77 – GUITAR LEGENDS
Keith Richards

84 – POP STARS
Kylie Minogue

71 – OPERA
Maria Callas

78 – FILM CHARACTERS
The Addams Family

85 – FASHION
Tom Ford

72 – FILM CHARACTERS
Marilyn Monroe in Some Like it Hot

79 – FASHION
Vivienne Westwood

86 – SPORT
John McEnroe (tennis)

73 – POLITICS
John F. Kennedy

80 – FASHION
Donatella Versace

87 – CHEFS
Jamie Oliver

88 – FILM COUPLES/FAMILY
Humphrey Bogart & Lauren Bacall

95 – MUSIC
Stevie Wonder

102 – COMEDY
Richard Pryor

89 – MUSIC
Krist Novoselic, Kurt Cobain & David Grohl of Nirvana

96 – FILM CHARACTERS
Al Pacino in Scarface

103 – MUSIC
Bob Dylan

90 – SPORT/FILM
Hulk Hogan (wrestling)

97 – FILM COUPLES
Clark Gable & Vivien Leigh in Gone With the Wind

104 – MUSIC
Barbra Streisand

91 – SPORT/FILM
Mr T (wrestling)

98 – FILM CHARACTERS
Liza Minnelli in Cabaret

105 – MUSIC
Barry, Robin & Maurice Gibb of The Bee Gees

92 – FILM COUPLES
Patrick Swayze & Jennifer Grey in Dirty Dancing

99 – COMEDY
Eddie Murphy

106 – FILM CHARACTERS
Robert Pattinson in Twilight

93 – FILM COUPLES
Leonardo DiCaprio & Kate Winslet in Titanic

100 – POETRY/THEATRE
William Shakespeare

107 – FILM CHARACTERS
Marlon Brando in The Godfather

94 – REVOLU-TIONARIES/ACTIVISTS
Martin Luther King

101 – OPERA
Luciano Pavarotti

108 – LIFESTYL GURU
Martha Stewart

109 – MUSIC
Brian May, Freddie
Mercury, John
Deacon & Roger
Taylor of Queen

116 – ART
Andy Warhol

**110 – TV SERIES
CHARACTERS**
Farrah Fawcett,
Kate Jackson &
Jaclyn Smith in
Charlie's Angels

117 – MUSIC
Florence Ballard,
Diana Ross & Mary
Wilson of The
Supremes

**111 – GUITAR
LEGENDS**
Eric Clapton

118 – MUSIC
Michael Bolton

**112 – TV SERIES
CHARACTERS**
Glee

119 – MUSIC
Tina Turner

113 – SPORT
Zinedine Zidane
(football)

120 – MUSIC
Rod Stewart

114 – SPORT
Serena & Venus
Williams (tennis)

121 – MUSIC
Prince

115 – CHEFS
Gordon Ramsay

I WOULD LIKE TO THANK
LAURENCE KING, ANGUS HYLAND, JO LIGHTFOOT, NINA CHAKRABARTI,
EFTHIMIS FILIPPOU, MELISSA DANNY, & SMITH, HELENA LEKKA,
MARY IKONIADOU, COMPANY, POLINA TABAKAKI, GABRIELE HERZOG,
BILLY KIOSOGLOU, CLARE SHILLAND, WOOD MCGRATH, BETH FENTON,
REBECCA DENNETT, AEMILIA MANIATAKI, MARIA ARGYROU,
VASSILIS MARMATAKIS, NATASA KOTSI, LILA KOTSI, MARIA TELONI,
ELENI TELONI, CHRISTOS VOUDASKAS, HELENA VOUDASKA,
AND FINALLY KYRIAKOS AND LIA CHRISTOFOROU.